3 4028 08619 3894
HARRIS COUNTY PUBLIC LIBRARY

P9-CLV-700

ANTI-BULLYING BASICS

BULLIED *by Friends*

WORLD
BOOK

A Scott Fetzer company
Chicago
worldbook.com

Staff

World Book, Inc.
233 North Michigan Avenue
Suite 2000
Chicago, Illinois, 60601 U.S.A.

For information about other World Book publications, visit our website at **www.worldbook.com** or call **1-800-967-5325.**

The contents of this book were reviewed by Kari A. Sassu, Ph.D., NCSP, assistant professor, Counseling and School Psychology Department, and coordinator, School Psychology Program, Southern Connecticut State University, New Haven, Connecticut.

Product development: Arcturus Publishing Ltd
Writer: Cath Senker
Editor and picture researcher: Nicola Barber
Designer: Ian Winton

Executive Committee

President
Donald D. Keller
Vice President and Editor in Chief
Paul A. Kobasa
Vice President, Sales and Marketing
Sean Lockwood
Vice President, International
Richard Flower
Controller
Anthony Doyle
Director, Human Resources
Bev Ecker

Editorial

Associate Director, Annuals and Topical Reference
Scott Thomas
Managing Editor, Annuals and Topical Reference
Barbara A. Mayes
Senior Editor
Christine Sullivan
Administrative Assistant
Ethel Matthews
Manager, Contracts & Compliance (Rights & Permissions)
Loranne K. Shields
Administrative Assistant
Gwen Johnson

Graphics and Design

Art Director
Tom Evans
Senior Designer
Don Di Sante
Media Researcher
Jeff Heimsath

Editorial Administration

Director, Systems and Projects
Tony Tills
Senior Manager, Publishing Operations
Timothy Falk

Manufacturing/Production

Director
Carma Fazio
Manufacturing Manager
Steven K. Hueppchen
Production/Technology Manager
Anne Fritzinger
Proofreader
Nathalie Strassheim

Marketing

Manager
Tamika Robinson
Marketing Specialist
Annie Suhy

Library of Congress Cataloging-in-Publication Data

Bullied by friends.
    pages cm. -- (Anti-bullying basics)
    Includes index.
    Summary: "A discussion of the problems young people face with peer pressure, which can lead to them taking risky behaviors and accepting bullying; contains advice and useful strategies for overcoming peer pressure"-- Provided by publisher.
    ISBN 978-0-7166-2072-3
    1. Bullying--Juvenile literature. 2. Peer pressure--Juvenile literature. I. World Book, Inc.
BF637.B85B8245 2014
302.34'3-dc23
                                        2013030501

Anti-Bullying Basics   Set ISBN: 978-0-7166 2070-9
Printed in China by PrintWORKS Global Services, Shenzhen, Guangdong
1st printing November 2013

Contents

What Is Bullying? 4

Bullying and the Problem of Peer Pressure 6

Negative Peer Pressure 8

Spoken and Unspoken Peer Pressure 10

In Class 12

Keeping Cool at School 14

The Need to Look Right 16

Dealing with Drinking 18

Staying Sober, Having Fun 20

The Smoking Habit 22

Staying Smoke-Free 24

Why Do People Take Illegal Drugs? 26

Top Tips to Resist Drugs 28

I Don't Have a Date! 30

Young, Gay, and Under Pressure 32

The Push to Have Sex 34

Committing Crime? 36

Offering a Helping Hand 38

Advice and Assistance 40

Resisting the Pressure to Bully 42

Additional Resources 44

Glossary 46

Index 47

Acknowledgments 48

What Is Bullying?

Bullying is unwanted, deliberately hurtful behavior that is repeated over a period of time. Bullying is often about an imbalance of power—bullies may use their physical strength, popularity, or something they know about another person to harm or control others.

Forms of bullying

Bullying can take many forms, including verbal, physical, social, and cyberbullying (a form of bullying on digital devices).

- Verbal bullying includes name-calling, teasing, inappropriate comments, threats, and abusive comments.
- Physical bullying includes hitting, kicking, spitting, tripping, and stealing or damaging possessions.
- Social bullying includes deliberately excluding someone from social events, spreading rumors about a person, and embarrassing or humiliating someone.
- Cyberbullying includes harassment and abuse via a cell phone, on social media sites, or online.

What bullying is not

Bullying is not:

- single occurrences of rejection, nastiness, or spite
- random acts of aggression
- one-time arguments or disagreements

All of these events can cause unhappiness. While falling out with friends or dealing with occasional disagreements may not be pleasant, they are a normal part of the process of learning and growing up. These occasional "dramas" in everyday life are very different from bullying, which is deliberate and repeated aggressive behavior that is intended to cause harm and unhappiness.

ABOUT THESE BOOKS

This series of books—*Anti-Bullying Basics*—
examines six different aspects of bullying:
bullying by groups, bullying by boys, bullying by
girls, bullying in cyberspace, bullying by friends,
and bullying to "fit in." Each book examines
the causes and effects of a particular type of
bullying and provides support and practical
advice for dealing with bullies. Bullying happens
everywhere in society: It often goes unchecked
because of the fear it creates, and because
people don't take it seriously. But with help, it
is always possible to stand up to bullies and to
break the cycle of bullying.

Why it's serious

Bullying is serious because it can have a damaging effect on the
person being bullied, on the person doing the bullying, and even on
the bystanders who witness incidents of bullying. Bullying creates a
climate of fear, and bystanders may be anxious that they will be next
on the bully's list of targets. The targets, the people who are being
bullied, are more likely to lack self-confidence, have low self-esteem,
have difficulty concentrating, and suffer from depression and anxiety.
People who bully are at greater risk than others of becoming involved
in violence and crime. Bullies also have a higher risk of struggling or
failing at their school studies. Young people who are both bullies and
bullied are at the highest risk of mental health problems later in life.
And, both bullies and their targets may have a more difficult time
forming healthy relationships as adults.

Bullying and the Problem of Peer Pressure

As children grow up and become increasingly independent, they like to hang out with people of their own age—classmates, teammates, friends from youth groups. People of roughly the same age and status are known as *peers,* and it's likely that they share many experiences and interests.

Peer pressure

Relationships with peers become extremely important as children develop and mature. It's quite natural for friends to compare the things they are doing or the things they have, and for friends to have a strong influence over each other.

The influence that comes from peers is called *peer pressure.* It can often come from a group, where the pressure is to fit in with a certain set of attitudes, behaviors, or beliefs. For example, your class may have a popular set of cool kids. Everyone inside the group feels the pressure to keep up the cool image. People outside experience pressure to be like the popular kids and to be liked by them. If you have a boyfriend or girlfriend, he or she may exert influence over you, too. You want to please this person. Everyone experiences peer pressure—not just young people. It can be both a positive and negative influence in life.

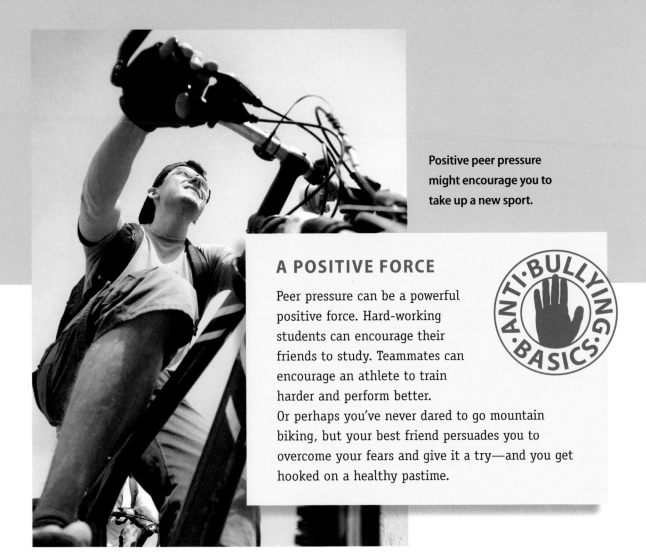

A POSITIVE FORCE

Peer pressure can be a powerful
positive force. Hard-working
students can encourage their
friends to study. Teammates can
encourage an athlete to train
harder and perform better.
Or perhaps you've never dared to go mountain
biking, but your best friend persuades you to
overcome your fears and give it a try—and you get
hooked on a healthy pastime.

ANTI·BULLYING·BASICS

Peer pressure and its connection to bullying

Many of the people involved in bullying are not bullies or
their targets—they are bystanders. People who stand and
watch while bullying from going on. Why do they just watch as
another person is teased, tormented, or physically harmed? One
explanation may be peer pressure. The desire to fit in, to seem
cool, is often a reason for people not to "get involved."

Learning how to resist peer pressure in a variety of ways
will help you to avoid risky behaviors that can harm you.
It will also allow you to become the person who *intervenes*
(steps in) when you see bullying. When you learn to make
choices based on what you want instead of trying to fit in, you
learn to say no to risky behaviors you don't want to engage in
and to behaviors that are morally wrong, such as bullying.

Negative Peer Pressure

Peer pressure can be a negative influence that can be very difficult to deal with. Peers may try to persuade you to do things you know you shouldn't or don't want to be part of.

Persuasion

Have friends ever tried to persuade you to do something you know your parents would oppose? They might have suggested you drink alcohol, or smoke, or take drugs. Maybe someone has asked you to lie on their behalf, saying they're staying at your house when in fact they are going to a party. It can be hard to withstand peer pressure in these situations.

Peer pressure to drink alcohol can be hard to withstand.

Gender pressure

Another example of negative peer pressure is the pressure to fit in with what is considered "normal" for your gender. Maybe all of your girlfriends are starting to dress up and wear makeup every day for class? They keep pushing you to do the same. But you're comfortable in sweatpants, sneakers, and a ponytail.

Why give in?

Negative peer pressure pushes you to do something that is not your choice and that you may know is wrong or bad for you. So why might you give in? Perhaps you want to be liked and to fit in, and you're scared you will be bullied or excluded if you don't *conform* (act like everyone else). You might want to try out the activity, even if it is risky. If you think "everybody" is doing it, you may simply go along with it.

If you do give in to peer pressure, you may feel sad, anxious, guilty, or annoyed with yourself afterward. This might make you determined not to fall for the same trick again. Being aware of negative peer pressure is important. It allows you to learn how to deal with peer pressure.

BULLYING Q & A

How do I know what's good and what's bad?

Q. How do I know the difference between good and bad peer pressure?

A. If you are being pressured into doing something illegal or that could harm you or others, it is negative peer pressure. It's also negative if it involves lying or sneaking around to avoid the consequences. But if the activity provides a positive new experience or could improve your health or grades, it's positive peer pressure. The best peer-pressure test is: How will it make you feel about yourself—better or worse?

She still wants to wear sneakers, while her friends like dressing up.

Spoken and Unspoken Peer Pressure

Peer pressure can take many different forms. Spoken peer pressure can range from subtle suggestion to threats and insults. Unspoken pressure, such as a person's behavior, can also be used to gain influence over peers.

Unspoken peer pressure can escalate into bullying.

Spoken peer pressure

Verbal peer pressure is the most direct form of peer pressure. The following examples move from peer pressure to bullying. Peer pressure might include giving a seemingly good reason to engage in an activity, such as "Come and drink with us—it'll be more fun than studying." The reason is designed to make an activity seem perfectly sensible, even if it isn't. Insulting comments, such as "Don't be such a loser!" move into the area of bullying. The bully insults you in the hope that you will feel bad enough to join in with whatever he or she wants you to do.

Threatening people with rejection with such comments as "We won't hang out with you if you don't . . ." are a further step on the bullying scale. Threats are a powerful form of pressure. People may say they'll drop you as a friend or spread nasty rumors about you if you don't do what they want. *Psychologists* (experts who study how people think and feel) call this type of bullying *relational aggression*. Relational aggression is an attempt to damage your friendships or your *status* (social standing) with your peers.

Unspoken peer pressure

The most common example of unspoken peer pressure is behavior that makes you feel left out. You see the popular group all laughing and joking—but you're not part of it. They throw you a glance to show that you are excluded. If this type of pressure affects you, it's time to find some friends who will make you feel secure and wanted.

SHUNNED BY CLASSMATES

In 8th grade, Colleen went through a lot of bullying—being excluded from social groups and being called names. She used to spend lunch and recess in the bathroom, many times crying. Some of her best friends turned against her, and she felt completely worthless. Colleen convinced herself there was something about her that made all of these people exclude her. She had a great family, however, who helped her to feel better about herself. In high school, she made a new group of friends and rarely saw the people from middle school who had made her so unhappy.

The peer-pressure test

These are all tricks you can spot. Once you're aware of them, you can figure out how to respond. First, apply the peer-pressure test: How would you feel about yourself if you gave in? If you decide to say "no," then do so firmly, using body language to make the point. Stand up straight and make eye contact. Explain how you feel, without making excuses. If you are having a hard time standing up to peer pressure or bullying on your own, ask a trusted adult for help on how to deal with the situation.

In Class

School can be a breeding ground for all kinds of negative peer pressure. There can be pressure to copy such bad behavior as skipping class, smoking, or drinking.

Pressure in class

Your peers may think it's uncool to study hard, and some of them may think it's daring to cut classes or cheat on tests. Everyone may say they love the class clown who cracks jokes, shows a lack of respect for the teacher, and misbehaves. It can be hard to stay focused at school when there is constant pressure to mess around.

It's hard to stay focused if your peers are always acting up in class.

Cliques

A clique is a small and exclusive group of friends, often with similar interests or tastes. Cliques can create a huge amount of pressure. It's normal to enjoy being part of a group for security and friendship (though it's fine if you don't). People sometimes form a clique because they share interests in certain activities, such as electronic gaming, sports, or music. There can be a lot of pressure within the clique to dress in a certain way, which can be hard if a person can't afford the clothes and accessories. And some cliques do everything together, inside and out of school. This can feel like being smothered by friends.

Bullying and exclusion

The problem with cliques is that they can become "closed" groups, with pressure to bully and exclude those outside the group. There may be pressure within the clique to follow a ringleader in being mean to a particular student, or excluding him or her. Members of the clique may tease the people they exclude, calling them names because they seem different in some way.

PRESSURE TO FIT IN

In Kayla's class there is a group of girls who are really into hair and jewelry and certain clothing labels. The only people who get to hang out with them are the ones who wear the "right" stuff.

Even then, they won't accept you if you're too tall or too fat. If you don't look like them, they ignore you, unless they're making fun of how you look. Kayla says it's best if they don't even know you exist.

ANTI·BULLYING ·BASICS·

If you want to hang out with this group,
you have to wear the "right" stuff.

Keeping Cool at School

Think carefully when your peer group misbehaves. Disrupting the class is no good for anyone, and skipping class will likely get you into trouble. Try to look beyond the pressure to follow the group and consider your future. If your friends don't like to study, seek out others who do—maybe at an after-class study group.

Try to stay focused at school.

In a group?

If you're in a group, don't worry if it's not the coolest or most popular one. If you love math, you'll be happier hanging out with others who love math. But whatever group you're in, make the effort to befriend others, too. It will help you develop new interests and friendships. Also, be sure you're not mean to others. There is no reason to shun or bully people not in your group.

Friendship group or clique? Try taking this test to see what your group is like:

• Do you feel accepted for who you are?

• Can you have your own opinion?

• Do you enjoy different types of activities together?

• Are people in your group expected to act alike? Dress alike? Think alike?

• Are people respectful of others both in and out of the group?

Outside the clique

What if you're experiencing unwelcome peer pressure from a clique? Try to keep out of their way. It helps if you have at least one other friend to spend time with, or you could seek out new activities to be with different people.

LONE WOLF

Jessie has always been independent—a lone wolf. He couldn't find a group where he fitted in, so he decided to form his own group. He started a creative writing club at his school, and now it's eight members strong! That's why he recommends making your own group. It will help you meet some like-minded people.

ANTI·BULLYING·BASICS

Make your own group with like-minded friends.

The Need to Look Right

As you grow up, it's likely you'll experience peer pressure to look "right." Although it's hard not to compare yourself with others, it's worth knowing that no one—not even the most attractive person you know—is entirely content with how they look.

Accept how you are

You can't change most aspects of your appearance, so try to accept them. Remember that eating a healthy diet and exercise will help you look your best.

Pressure for possessions

The pressure to own the latest clothing, electronic goods, and other accessories can be as stressful as the pressure to look attractive. If you feel the desperate urge to possess an item you can't afford, think carefully. Is it a fad that will be forgotten by next month, or will it be long-lasting? Do you really need the designer version or would the regular one be fine? If it's not a fad or extremely costly, ask a parent for support. If they can afford it, maybe they could buy it for your birthday or in exchange for your helping them out.

Shopping is fun, but peer pressure to "look right" can be stressful.

Be alternative

Another option is to develop your own independent style by hunting bargain vintage items at thrift stores and garage sales. Or you could arrange to share possessions with siblings or good friends. Most importantly, do your best not to judge others on how they look. Take opportunities to talk to others with a different style—look beyond the appearance and accessories to the person within.

STANDING UP FOR HERSELF

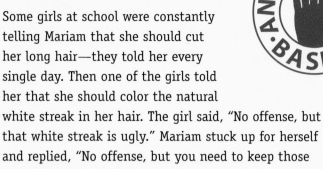

Some girls at school were constantly telling Mariam that she should cut her long hair—they told her every single day. Then one of the girls told her that she should color the natural white streak in her hair. The girl said, "No offense, but that white streak is ugly." Mariam stuck up for herself and replied, "No offense, but you need to keep those thoughts to yourself!"

She's happy with her own look.

Dealing with Drinking

Did anyone ever offer you an alcoholic drink? It may seem like "everyone's doing it," but in fact, most young people don't drink. Anyway, it is illegal to drink if you are under 21.

Friends who drink

Peer pressure plays an important role in underage drinking. A study by researchers at Columbia University shows that kids are six times more likely to drink alcohol if their friends do. So if you hang out with drinkers, it's difficult to resist the pressure.

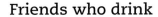

Direct pressure

You may experience direct pressure from friends who drink. They might give reasons, such as "you'll enjoy yourself more." They may bully and insult you, calling you childish, or saying that "you're boring if you don't."

Some teens may think it's cool to drink beer, but it is illegal for anyone under age 21.

Indirect pressure

You might come under indirect pressure, too. If you're at a party where alcohol is available, you might feel awkward if you don't drink. It may seem like everyone else is drinking and having a great time, so you'll feel left out if you don't. Drinking alcohol may feel right at the time, even though you know you shouldn't do it. It's a health risk and illegal if you're under 21.

BULLYING Q & A

Should I hang out with them?

Q. I moved to a new neighborhood with my family, and I have no friends to hang out with. I'm really lonely. Last week I saw some kids my age in the local park hanging out together and drinking. They seemed friendly, even though they drink and I'm not interested in alcohol. I'm so bored at home alone. Should I go spend some time with them?

···

A. It's not wise to join this group, even if you're desperate for company. These kids may put pressure on you to drink with them, which involves risks to your health. Also, drinking in public could get you all in trouble with the police. Why not look for activities in your new neighborhood and school? An interesting pastime will help you to make new friends.

Staying Sober, Having Fun

There are plenty of ways to avoid drinking without losing face. The ideal is to keep away from situations where people drink alcohol by finding activities with other friends. But you may feel you're missing out on the big parties your peers enjoy. If you build up the confidence, you can go to events where some young people drink alcohol—but stay sober yourself.

Enjoying the company of friends—without alcohol.

Plan your response

Planning is the key to staying alcohol-free. Think up some good responses to use when you're offered drinks. If you feel able to be honest about not wanting to drink, that's great. Be clear but not pushy; this is not the time to talk about how dumb it is to drink. Remember that people can become aggressive when they've had alcohol. A firm "no thanks" is perfect. When you do this, you are learning to develop your own "voice," learning to state what you want without fear of what others think. It's a long road and it takes practice, but you can get there.

Come up with reasons

If a straight "no" seems difficult, see if you can come up with a good reason to refuse—perhaps you have practice for a sport the following morning and your coach will cut you from the team if you are caught drinking. It can be helpful to bring your own soft drinks to the party so people can see you already have a drink.

BULLYING Q & A

How do I deal with bad-influence friends?

Q. Kaci, 12, asked on the PBS Kids' forum: Have you ever had a friend who you knew was a bad influence on you?

....

A. Yeah, sure. Most of my friends are what people would call a "bad influence." I have friends who smoke and drink. But we're in high school so . . . parents kind of expect it and usually don't find out or we don't tell them. I'm smart enough to know not to drink and smoke—so I don't.

Get a ride home

If you're concerned that these options won't work or are anxious about being at a party that might get out of hand, arrange beforehand with a parent to bring you home, or call home and ask someone to pick you up. And, one of the most important rules at such a party is: *Never get in a car if the person driving has had even one alcoholic drink, and never drive if you have had anything alcoholic to drink yourself.*

Be smart—even if your friends drink alcohol and smoke, you don't have to.

The Smoking Habit

Peer pressure is a major reason why young people start smoking. Despite all the information about the dangers of smoking, some people still see smoking as cool.

The facts are:

- The younger people are when they start smoking, the more likely they are to develop a serious, smoking-related disease.

- People who start smoking before 16 are twice as likely to continue smoking when they become adults.

Few smokers

This is another case where peer pressure can make you think that everybody's smoking—but only a small minority actually do. According to the U.S. Centers for Disease Control and Prevention (CDC), only 4 percent of middle schoolers smoked in 2011.

Remember, only a few young people actually try smoking. Most young people resist the pressure to smoke.

BULLYING Q & A

Why did I do it?

Q. I am 11 years old. . . After school, I usually go to the park with my friends, but recently one of my friends snuck out some cigarettes and a lighter from her sister. She lit a cigarette and smoked it around me and our other friends. She was calling me names, saying I was a "chicken" for not trying it. This made me feel bad. . . so I tried just one puff and hated it. I felt so disappointed with myself for giving in to her. What should I do now?

A. I can understand why you are upset—your friend has been unkind and put you under pressure. Don't worry about trying the cigarette. You have learned from the experience, and now you're standing up for yourself. It's good that you have looked for help. Why not talk to your other friends about the girl who is smoking and see how they feel, or to a parent or other trusted adult? Try some advice websites for helping to deal with peer pressure.

PLEASE
NO SMOKING!

Staying Smoke-Free

As with alcohol, it's helpful to prepare your response in case you are offered cigarettes. Remember—it's up to you whether you smoke or not. You don't have to explain your reasons to anyone. A firm "no thanks" is all you need.

A firm refusal should be enough if you are offered a cigarette.

Good excuses

Sometimes, it's hard to just say "no." You could try one of these replies:

- "I'm allergic to cigarette smoke."
- "My parents will punish me if I smell of smoke."
- "I'm trying to help my parents quit."
- "I just quit smoking."

Real friends?

If your friends pressure you to smoke, then what kind of friends are they? You don't need friends who expect you always to do what they do. Maybe they are insecure and trying to make you feel small to make themselves feel better. Whatever the reason, if the pressure doesn't stop, you may want to seek new companions.

Peer pressure can prevent smoking

Interestingly, positive peer pressure can discourage young people from smoking. As part of a school program in the United Kingdom, 12- to 13-year-olds were asked to select the most popular students in their class. These students trained to become "peer supporters" who learned about the dangers and costs of smoking. They then used their influence in a positive way. It was found that children in the class of a peer supporter were less likely to start smoking than those in a class without. The program was particularly successful in poor areas, which have higher levels of smoking. In the United States, the Positive Behavioral Interventions and Supports program through the U.S. Department of Education works in much the same way. The program works to encourage all members of a school community (adults and kids) to support and reinforce each other's positive behaviors.

TRYING OUT SMOKING

Rahul has smoked before. He did it a couple of times purely out of curiosity, wondering what was so exciting about cigarettes. From his experience, Rahul decided that cigarettes taste bad and make you light-headed. He knows that after a while they can seriously start to affect your body. Rahul figures the best way to resist peer pressure to try smoking is to not hang around those kids that do smoke. As he says, "Trust me, you'll still be cool without the cigarette."

Antismoking posters during National Kick Butt Day

Why Do People Take Illegal Drugs?

There are many kinds of illegal drugs, including marijuana, cocaine, and heroin. And, some people abuse prescription drugs—such as painkillers, tranquilizers, and sedatives—for nonmedical reasons. Marijuana is the most commonly used recreational drug, and though some U.S. states have legalized the use of marijuana, it remains illegal for people under 18.

You can never be sure of the effect that drugs will have on you.

Risks

Taking any drug involves risks. Even drugs prescribed by a doctor may cause side effects. Illegal drugs are often mixed with other substances, so you can never be sure how they will affect you.

Reasons

Young people generally overestimate the amount of drug-taking their peers are doing. In fact, the majority of high-school students have never tried illegal drugs. Those who take drugs have different reasons. Some like the element of risk and enjoy the feelings they get from drugs. Others are feeling bad about themselves and take drugs to try to escape the problems. Yet the effects of drugs are always temporary.

Direct and indirect pressure

Young people may experience direct pressure to take drugs from peers, but more often it is from older friends, siblings, or a boy- or girlfriend. Indirect pressure exists, too. It may appear attractive to take drugs because the kids who are considered cool do it. If you're experiencing peer pressure, remember that there are many other kids like you who avoid drugs.

BULLYING Q & A

Will he ditch me?

Q. At college I met this boy. He smokes weed quite a bit, and we were talking about it and stuff. He seems to think I smoke weed, and I have never done it in my life! We are meeting up today to "get high." But I know I have an excuse (family dinner). I don't want him to find out I don't smoke and ditch me because of it. He seems really nice. What should I do?

···

A. If this boy really is a good person, he won't pressure you to do something you're not comfortable with. And if the relationship is going to develop, you might want to explain that you love spending time together, but you'd prefer it if drugs were not involved.

A police officer examines a marijuana plant.

Top Tips to Resist Drugs

If you're feeling under pressure to take drugs, try to take some time out to think through the consequences. To feel accepted today, you could be making a choice that will have a terrible effect on you for the rest of your life.

There are ways to get a natural "high" without using drugs.

Before you give in to pressure to take drugs, consider:

- What are the likely effects of the drugs and could they harm you physically?
- What will happen if the police catch you?
- What could be the long-term effects on your health, family, and relationships?

Tackling the pressure

Now consider why people are pressuring you. Perhaps they want approval for their behavior by involving you. If they're acting like this, are they genuine friends? Once you have thought this through, think about tactics to resist the pressure. The best way is a firm "no thanks," rather than making excuses, which can allow people to try to persuade you. If that's difficult, try these suggestions:

- "If my parents find out, they'll ground me for sure."
- "I have a test tomorrow—I can't use drugs today."
- "It's illegal and I don't want to get into trouble."

Find an ally

See if you can find a friend who also resists drugs. It's easier to say "no" with another person standing alongside you. If you need more help, ask a parent or another trusted adult. It may be useful to role-play your responses to pressure about taking drugs. You could also arrange with a parent to bring you home if you find yourself in a situation where others are taking drugs.

New activities

You could try suggesting other activities to your friends that don't involve drugs. If this doesn't work, perhaps you could find a new pastime yourself and meet new people.

NAOMI'S TACTICS

Naomi feels that peer pressure is a growing problem that is sometimes hard to avoid. She usually just walks away or ignores it. If friends try to persuade her to do something she doesn't want to do, she thinks about finding better friends. Anyone knows a good friend wouldn't force you to do something. Naomi thinks teens everywhere should be really aware of who they hang out with because otherwise they may be pushed into risky decisions that are wrong for them.

I Don't Have a Date!

Is everyone around you talking about dating? Perhaps several of your friends already have partners. They are so excited, and all they can talk about is each other! You may feel that you, too, should be in a relationship.

Putting pressure on yourself

People frequently put pressure on themselves; they feel they are not normal because they don't have a girl- or boyfriend. But maybe you're not ready. You're happy being with your friends, and you simply aren't attracted to anyone in your grade. This is absolutely fine. There is no rush to start having relationships. Everyone is different, and many young teens prefer to wait until they are older.

Focus on friendship

To resist the pressure, focus on building friendships. Good friendships are the basis of good relationships. If you're able to make and stay friends with people of both sexes, then you have a good chance of making successful relationships when you're ready.

It may feel as if everyone around you is one half of a couple.

BULLYING Q & A

Why don't I have a boyfriend?

Q. I'm 13 and I haven't had a boyfriend yet. All of my friends have and at school they are all there, and I'm the only single person. What's wrong with me?

....

A. Nothing! But it's tough when it feels like you're the only single person. Remember that there's no point going out with someone simply because you want a boyfriend. If your friends are busy with their boyfriends, it could be the right time to break out and try a new activity with different people. Make the effort to get to know boys and girls. You'll have fun, and no doubt at some point you'll meet someone you'd like to date.

Young, Gay, and Under Pressure

As you go through puberty, the changes in your body bring new sexual feelings. It can be a very confusing time. You may have sexual thoughts about people of the other gender, the same gender, or both. These things are perfectly normal. If you're interested in someone of the same sex, it doesn't mean that you are definitely gay. Similarly, you might be interested in someone of the opposite sex and not be *straight* (heterosexual).

Discovering your sexuality

Over time, you will work out whether you are gay, straight, or bisexual (attracted to both sexes). The letters LGBT are used to describe people who are "*l*esbian, *g*ay, *b*isexual, or *t*ransgender."

LGBT teens

Peer pressure can be particularly hard for young LGBT people. It may seem like everyone is expected to be straight. LGBT teens can feel left out when their straight friends are talking about dating and romance. Many hear negative comments about their sexual preference and feel pressure to hide the fact that they are gay.

A parade in Toronto, Canada, celebrates the LGBT population in the city.

Seeking support

Resisting the pressure is easier if you have supportive friends or family members. However, even though acceptance of LGBT people in society is growing, many people are in families or communities where such differences are not tolerated. In that case, look for a trusted adult or a support group that can help or talk privately to a counselor.

GAY-FRIENDLY SCHOOLS

LGBT teens have a difficult time in high school. These teens are far more likely to experience harassment and bullying than heterosexual kids. They are also much more likely to miss class because they feel unsafe at school; truancy leads to LGBT kids having higher dropout levels in high school. In New York City, there is a special school that was opened to create a friendly environment for LGBT kids. Harvey Milk High School was opened as a private school in 1985, and it became accredited as a public school in 2003. The school has a graduation rate of 95 percent, much higher than the citywide average of 52 percent. In 2013, public school officials in Chicago recommended that such a school be opened in the Second City, as well.

The Push to Have Sex

Are you receiving conflicting messages about sex? Your friends may be persuading you to have sex, or a boy- or girlfriend may be encouraging you. On the other hand, your parents might believe that you should wait until you're older, and the law in most states says you need to be at least 16 years old. So what do you do?

Dealing with friends

Note that many teens lie and say they're having sex when they're not! In fact, most people wait until they are older. You are the only person who can decide the right time for you—it's not up to your friends.

Pressure from a partner

Here are some possible responses to pressure from a boy- or girlfriend:

- "Don't you like me?"
  Reply: "Yes, of course, but let's get to know each other better."

- "Let's get it over with."
  Reply: "It'll be better if we wait until we're both ready."

There's no point having sex just to be able to say you've done it.

Don't let anyone pressure you to have sex before you're ready.

Am I ready?

Before you start having sex, it's vital to talk to the other person about contraception and the risks of sexually transmitted diseases (STDs).

If you're not prepared to do this, you're not ready to have sex.

BULLYING Q & A

Why are they pressuring me?

Q. I just met this guy, we take the bus together after school . . .
he's 15 and I'm 13. I have loads of friends on the bus, but they
don't act like they're my friends—they keep pressuring my
friend and me to kiss and hug and to hold hands. We do hug,
but that's it. I don't want to go too fast. Am I doing
something wrong?

....

A. No! It's great you have this new relationship and you are
sensible enough to take it slowly. Try talking to your friends
and explain that the pressure they're putting on you is hurtful
and could spoil your relationship. If they are real friends,
they will leave you and your boyfriend alone.

Committing Crime?

Peer pressure can lead some young people to commit such crimes as shoplifting and vandalism—things they might never consider if they were alone.

Shoplifting could get you into serious trouble.

Why do people shoplift?

All kinds of people shoplift—most are casual shoplifters who spot an opportunity. Among young people, there can be pressure to seem cool, daring, or rebellious. Alternatively, teens may feel peer pressure to own costly items they cannot afford.

Persuaded by friends

Friends may encourage you, saying it's simple, and no one will know. You may feel like a coward if you refuse. Yet you could easily be caught by the store detective. Then you're in trouble with the police.

Vandalism

Similar pressures lead people to vandalism. Perhaps your group is out and about and bored. Someone brings out a spray can and dares you to spray paint a garbage can or mailbox. There's no one around, and they reassure you that you'll get away with it.

Go with your instincts

To resist these kinds of pressures, go with your gut instinct. You feel uncomfortable and you know it's wrong. Explain to your friends why you don't want to be involved. If they still pressure you to do things you know to be wrong, avoid hanging around with them.

PRESSURE TO SHOPLIFT

Ryan was at a large store, and his girlfriend convinced him to shoplift some makeup for her. He had taken it out of the package and put it in his back pocket. Ryan was stopped at the register when he was about to walk out, and was accused of stealing. Ryan denied it, but he was told, "Well, it's in your back pocket." And it was. A staff member took him back to the security camera room and took down his personal information. His parents had to come and pick him up at the store. Ryan had never felt so miserable and ashamed.

Can you say no if someone dares you to paint graffiti on a wall?

Offering a Helping Hand

If a friend is experiencing peer pressure, allow them to express their feelings without interrupting or judging. Maybe you can help them to avoid a difficult situation. For example, if a group is pressuring someone to smoke, and you're at the same event too, you can say, "We have to leave now—let's go." It's far easier for two people to resist pressure than one person alone.

Be a good friend—
let a friend talk
about her problems.

Ask advice

If you're not sure how to help a friend, talk to a parent or another trusted adult. If they can't help, at least they will have ideas about who to ask. It may be a school counselor, a school psychologist, or a law enforcement officer (depending on the situation).

Positive peer pressure

As a group, you and your friends can exert positive peer pressure. For example, you can keep an eye out for bullying behavior and help the victims. You can set a good example by respecting each other and treating people fairly. You can lead the way by becoming involved in such positive activities as sports, music, or volunteer work.

Peer education

Peer education is positive peer pressure. In Norway, youth volunteers pass on the safer sex message through a program in schools and youth clubs. No adults attend the sessions, and the teenagers feel comfortable asking questions and engaging in discussion.

BULLYING Q & A

How can I help my sister?

Q. My younger sister and I are constantly arguing. I feel as though she's getting in with the wrong crowd. I'm worried about her! She is 13 . . . and they encourage her to do things she shouldn't. What can I do?

....

A. When you were 13, how would you have felt if someone had told you who you could and couldn't be friends with? The most useful thing you can do is become a pillar of support in her life. Let her know, in your super-cool big sister way, that you're there for her when she needs you. You might not be able to stop her getting into trouble, but you'll be able to help her out if she does, and she'll likely learn from the experience. If she's engaging in truly risky or harmful behavior, however, then you need to tell an adult.

Working as part of a team in a community project is a great example of positive peer pressure.

Advice and Assistance

What if you've tried all the tips in this book but you need further help? Sometimes, you can't solve problems alone or even with your friends' help. There are several other options.

Talking to a counselor can help resolve your problems.

Someone to talk to

You could try talking about the issue with a parent. Even if you feel that they don't understand you, remember that they are older and more experienced than you and may have useful suggestions. If you can't talk to a parent, perhaps another close relative could offer some advice. At school, a teacher, staff member, or guidance counselor might lend a listening ear. Perhaps there are peer counselors—people your age who are trained to help young people to sort out problems. If you are a member of a faith group, try talking to the faith leader at your church, temple, or mosque.

Therapists and helplines

If talking in this way is not possible or does not work, why not seek professional support from a therapist? Therapy is a widely accepted way of dealing with personal problems. The therapist is completely separate from your life and unbiased, and your conversations will be completely confidential. Another option is to call a helpline or contact a counselor through a youth support website—see pages 44-45 for resources. These services are also completely confidential.

SAMIRA TURNED HER LIFE AROUND

When she was 15, Samira made some pretty bad decisions. She started to drink and go to parties to make herself feel "cooler" and "prettier." After a while, it spun out of control. She was getting so drunk she had no control over what she was doing and was making mistakes that made her feel worse about herself. Of course, the drinking didn't fix anything, and when Samira's problems remained, she stopped eating because she hoped that "being skinny" would make people like and accept her more. Eventually, Samira's doctor and parents intervened, and she began to realize that she didn't need to drink or starve herself for people to like her.

Is there a family member you could turn to?

Resisting the Pressure to Bully

You've read about a number of situations that are about peer pressure, and you've been given suggestions on how to resist falling into the peer-pressure trap. Now, how can you relate this to bullying?

Bullying to stay with the "in" group

Have your friends or acquaintances ever bullied someone while you were around? Maybe you felt terrible as you watched another person be hurt or humiliated, but you did nothing. You were afraid to speak up for fear your friends would stop liking you. Or, maybe you even feared they might turn on you. What can you do now?

- Even if you did not bully with your friends, and even if you did not laugh at the situation, just by watching you gave the sign that you approve of the bullying when you did not intervene.

- Try to make *amends* (make it up) for what you've done to the person who was bullied. Apologize to him or her and let them know how sorry you are that you did nothing at the time to help.

- Tell your friends who were actively bullying that you feel it was wrong and you won't stand by and let it happen any more. If that causes this group of friends to reject you, consider this: Bullies are not very good friends. Over time, you need to try to make better friends who can be trusted,

You can use peer pressure as a force for good to stand up to bullying.

You can make a difference

Studies have shown that when bystanders become involved to stop bullying, more than half of the time the bullying is stopped within 10 seconds. Further, you are a peer to the bully. The very peer pressure we have discussed in this book means that when you intervene with a bully, your intervention is more effective than that of an adult. Peer pressure can be used to good ends or bad. Make sure you're using your influence for the good.

PEER PRESSURE FOR GOOD

Anne walked down the hall at her school and ran into a large group of kids in a circle. When she got closer, she realized they were all watching the school bully, Rick, torment Jon. Anne had always been a little afraid of Rick. But, she felt really sorry for Jon. She was shaking inside, but she decided to try to intervene. She looked around at the people in the group and said, "This is stupid! Why are we all standing around watching this? Let's go!" She grabbed Jon by the arm and quickly walked with him to a place that she knew would be more crowded and where teachers would likely be present. She got Jon away from Rick. Later, other bystanders told Anne how much they wished they had been brave enough to do what she did. Anne decided to form an anti-bullying club that could encourage people to come forward and intervene when they saw bullying. The group practices by role-playing what to say when they see a bully tormenting someone. All of the club members are less afraid and more confident about what to do when they see bullying.

Use the power of a group to learn how to withstand bullying.

Additional Resources

Websites

http://www.anti-bullyingalliance.org/
A United Kingdom-based alliance of organizations that works to stop bullying and create safer environments.

http://www.bullying.org
A Canadian organization that provides educational programs and resources to individuals, families, educational institutions, and organizations.

http://www.bullypolice.org
A U.S. watchdog organization advocating for bullied children and reporting on state anti-bullying laws.

http://www.cdc.gov/bam/life/index.html
A Centers for Disease Control and Prevention (CDC) site for young adults about dealing with bullying, peer pressure, and stress.

http://www.thecoolspot.gov/pressures.asp
A site created by the U.S. National Institute on Alcohol Abuse and Alcoholism (NIAAA) for kids 11-13 years old.

https://www.facebook.com/safety/bullying
A campaign by Facebook and other sponsors asking everyone to show their support and spread the word against bullying. This page also has advice for people receiving abusive posts on Facebook.

http://www.itgetsbetter.org/
What began as a single YouTube video by author Dan Savage that encouraged young LGBT youth to tough it out through school, is now a website featuring thousands of videos made by youths and by celebrities attesting that life gets easier for LGBT people in adulthood.

http://www.ncpc.org/topics/bullying
A National Crime Prevention Council website, includes a page about girls and bullying.

http://www.nobully.com
An organization that helps schools to implement an anti-bullying program.

http://www.pacer.org/bullying/
PACER's National Bullying Prevention Center unites, engages, and educates communities nationwide to address bullying through creative, relevant, and interactive resources. PACER's bullying prevention resources are designed to benefit all students, including students with disabilities.

http://pbskids.org/itsmylife/
PBS advice site about issues that include family, friends, school, and emotions.

http://solutionsforbullying.com/Associations.html
Resources for parents, teachers, and other professionals listing organizations in different countries as a starting point for getting help.

http://www.stopbullying.gov/
A U.S. Department of Health & Human Services website with lots of information for kids, teens, parents, and educators.

http://www.violencepreventionworks.org/
A site for the Olweus Bullying Prevention Program, an American program that has been proven to reduce bullying in schools.

Books

How to Beat Physical Bullying (Beating Bullying series) by Alexandra Handon-Harding (Rosen Central, 2013)

Bullies, Cyberbullies and Frenemies (Teen Life Confidential series) by Michelle Elliott (Wayland, 2013)

Bullying (Teen Issues series) by Lori Hile (Heinemann 2012)

Bullying Under Attack: True Stories Written by Teen Victims, Bullies & Bystanders by Stephanie Meyer, John Meyer, Emily Sperber and Heather Alexander (Health Communications, Inc., 2013)

The Bullying Workbook for Teens: Activities to Help You Deal with Social Aggression and Cyberbullying by Raychelle Cassada Lohmann and Julia V. Taylor (New Harbinger Publications, 2013)

Confessions of a Former Bully by Trudy Ludwig (Tricycle Press, 2010)

The Courage to Be Yourself: True Stories by Teens About Cliques, Conflicts, and Overcoming Peer Pressure edited by Al Desetta and Educators for Social Responsibility (Free Spirit Publishing, 2005)

The Drama Years: Real Girls Talk About Surviving Middle School – Bullies, Brands, Body Image, and More by Haley Kilpatrick and Whitney Joiner (Free Press, 2012)

Friendship Troubles (A Smart Girl's Guide series) by Patti Kelley Criswell (American Girl Publishing, revised edition, 2013)

A Guys' Guide to Conflict/A Girls' Guide to Conflict (Flip-It-Over Guides to Teen Emotions) by Jim Gallagher and Dorothy Kavanaugh (Enslow Publishers, 2008)

Hot Issues, Cool Choices: Facing Bullies, Peer Pressure, Popularity, and Put-downs by Sandra Mcleod Humphrey (Prometheus Books, 2007)

lol...OMG!: What Every Student Needs to Know About Online Reputation Management, Digital Citizenship, and Cyberbullying by Matt Ivester (Serra Knight Publishing, 2011)

Online Bullying (Teen Mental Health series) by Peter Ryan (Rosen 2012)

Peer Pressure (Issues that Concern You series) edited by Lorraine Savage (Greenhaven Press, 2009)

Peer Pressure (Tough Topics series) by Elizabeth Raum (Heinemann Library, 2008)

Physical Bullying (Take a Stand Against Bullying series) by Jennifer Rivkin (Crabtree Publishing, 2013)

Queen Bees and Wannabes by Rosalind Wiseman (Piatkus 2002; rev. edition, Three Rivers Press, 2009)

Teen Cyberbullying Investigated: Where Do Your Rights End and Consequences Begin? by Thomas A. Jacobs (Free Spirit Publishing, 2010)

Helplines (USA)

Boys Town National Hotline:
1-800-448-3000 (available to all children; toll- free)

Child-Help USA:
1-800-422-4453 (24-hour toll-free)

National Suicide Prevention Lifeline:
1-800-273-TALK (1-888-628-9454, for Spanish-speaking callers; 24-hour toll-free)

Glossary

anti-bullying policies an agreed upon set of rules or actions to stop bullying

birth order a person's age in relation to the ages of his or her siblings (for example, being the youngest or oldest child in a family); psychologists believe birth order has an effect on personality

bystander someone who watches an event but who does not intervene

cyberbullying using such information technologies as e-mail, cell phones, and instant messaging to send harmful messages

desensitized having become accustomed to hurtful behavior

direct aggression openly aggressive behavior, such as kicking, hitting, or name-calling

eating disorder an illness related to ideas and behaviors about food and body image

exclusion being deliberately left out

gay homosexual; feeling sexually attracted to a person of the same sex (gay is a term more commonly used for men than women)

gender group a set of people of the same sex

hazing initiation ceremonies that can often be dangerous and abusive in nature

homophobia a fear of, or prejudice against, people who are homosexuals

indirect aggression a kind of quiet and sneaky aggressive behavior; it could involve such actions as spreading rumors or blaming a target for something he or she did not do

isolation feeling apart from or unlike other people

lesbian a woman who is sexually attracted to women

LGBT initials that stand for lesbian, gay, bisexual, and transgender

peer pressure feeling that you should do, think, or say something because that's what others your age are doing

relational aggression a type of bullying in which the bully tries to harm the target by damaging the target's friendships or lowering the target's social status

sibling rivalry fighting, disagreements, and competition between siblings (brothers and/ or sisters)

social status how popular a person is, usually defined by the people around them

transgender a person who does not identify with the gender assigned to them at birth; for example, someone born as a male child may grow up feeling female and wear clothing and take on behaviors associated with female children

Index

alcohol 8, 18-19, 20-21, 24, 41
anxiety 5, 8, 21

boyfriends 6, 26-27, 30-31,
    34-35
bullies 5, 10, 42, 43
bullying
    targets of 5, 7, 11, 38,
       42, 43
bystanders 5, 7, 42, 43

Chicago 33
cliques 12, 13, 14
cocaine 26
conforming 8
counselors 32, 38, 40
crime 5, 36-37
cyberbullying 4, 5

dating 30-31, 32
depression 5
drinking 8, 10, 12, 18-19, 20-
    21, 41
drugs 8, 26-27, 28-29

exclusion 4, 8, 10, 11, 12

fads 16
friendship groups 14, 15, 19
friendships 6, 10, 12, 14, 30

gay people 32-33
girlfriends 6, 26, 30-31, 34-35,
    37
Harvey Milk High
    School 33
helplines 40
heroin 26

intervention 7, 41, 42-43

LGBT 32-33

marijuana 26-27

name-calling 4, 11, 12, 23
New York City 33

peer pressure
    and bullying 7
    dealing with 38-39,
       40-41
    definition 6
    in school 12-13, 14-15
    negative 6, 8-9, 12
    positive 6, 9, 24, 38
    resisting 7, 14, 16,
       20-21, 24-25, 28-29,
       42-43
    spoken 10
    standing up to 29
    test 11
    to "look right" 12, 16-17
    to commit crime 36-37
    to date 30-31
    to drink 18-19, 20-21
    to have sex 34-35
    to smoke 22-23, 24-25
    to take drugs 26-27,
       28-29
    unspoken 10
peer support 24
physical bullying 4, 7
Positive Behavioral
    Interventions and Supports
    program 24
prescription drugs 26

psychologists 10, 38
puberty 32

relational aggression 10
role-playing 28, 43
rumors 4, 10

safer sex 38
school 11, 12-13, 14-15, 17,
    21, 24, 33, 38, 40, 43
self-esteem 5
sex 32, 34-35, 38
sexually transmitted diseases
    (STDs) 34
shoplifting 36, 37
siblings 16, 26
smoking 8, 12, 21, 22-23, 24-
    25, 27, 38

teasing 4, 7, 12
transgender 32
truancy 33

vandalism 36, 37
verbal bullying 4, 10

websites 23, 40

Acknowledgments

Cover photo: Corbis Images (Ocean)
Back cover photo: Shutterstock (East)

Alamy:
8 (Angela Hampton Picture Library), 10-11 and 26 (Ace Stock Limited), 12-13 (MBI), 14 and 18 (Image Source), 15 (PhotoAlto sas), 22 (Bubbles Photolibrary), 25 (ZUMA Press, Inc.), 33 (Maciej Dakowicz), 34 (Design Pics Inc.), 37 (Andrey Guryanov), 39 (Jim West), 40 (Lisa F. Young).

Corbis:
16 (Rick Gomez/Blend Images), 23 (Roy McMahon), 27 (Phil Schermeister), 41 (Laura Doss/Image Source).

Shutterstock:
4-5 and 42 (oliveromg), 6 (Zurijeta), 7 (YanLev), 9 (Devon Anne), 11 (Piyato), 13 (Mandy Godbehear), 17 (Masson), 19 (Victoria Andreas), 20 (Lucky Business), 21 (Samuel Borges Photography), 24 (Dani Vincek), 28 (lev radin), 29 (l i g h t p o e t), 30 (Poznyakov), 31 (2xSamara.com), 32 (rmnoa357), 35 (Pressmaster), 36 (Lisa S.), 38 (Martin Novak), 43 (Monkey Business Images).